BLACK
ACHIEVEMENTS
IN MUSIC

CELEBRATING LOUIS ARMSTRONG, BEYONCÉ, AND MORE

ELLIOTT SMITH
CICELY LEWIS, EXECUTIVE EDITOR

Lerner Publications ◆ Minneapolis

LETTER FROM CICELY LEWIS

Dear Reader,

As a girl, I wanted to be like Oprah Winfrey. She is a Black woman from Mississippi like me who became an award-winning actor, author, and businessperson. Oftentimes, history books leave out the accomplishments and contributions of people of color. When you

CICELY LEWIS

see someone who looks like you and has a similar background excelling at something, it helps you to see yourself be great.

I created Read Woke to amplify the voices of people who are often underrepresented. These books bring to light the beauty, talent, and integrity of Black people in music, activism, sports, the arts, and other areas. As you read, think about why it's important to celebrate Black excellence and the achievements of all people regardless of race, gender, or status. How did the people mentioned succeed despite barriers placed on them? How can we use these stories to inspire others?

Black excellence is everywhere in your daily life. I hope these people inspire you to never give up and continue to let your light shine.

With gratitude,

Cicely Lewis

TABLE OF CONTENTS

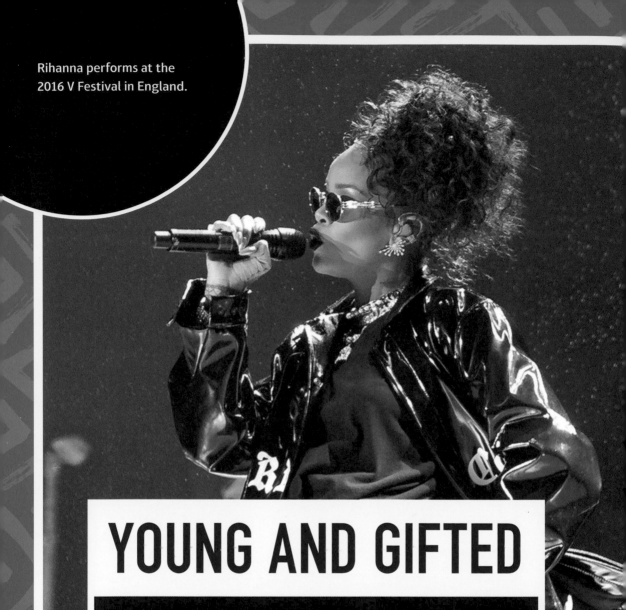

Rihanna performs at the 2016 V Festival in England.

YOUNG AND GIFTED

Discovered by a record producer at fifteen, Rihanna has become the second-best-selling female artist of all time. The singer, actor, and businessperson from Barbados has released many popular albums. Her music blends genres, including pop and R&B (rhythm & blues).

She won her ninth Grammy at the 2018 Grammy Awards. She sang "Loyalty" with the influential rapper Kendrick Lamar. Grammy Awards are given for achievement in music. Rihanna also won Grammys for her hits like "Umbrella" and "We Found Love." Rihanna shows how hard work and talent can pay off.

This book will explore Black excellence throughout a wide variety of music. Not every influential artist is highlighted here, but the artists you will read about are among those who have helped shape or innovate the industry and inspire its next generation.

Rihanna is a successful businessperson and the founder of Fenty Beauty. Here she is pictured in 2017.

Nat King Cole, the singer of hits like "L-O-V-E" and "Smile," puts on a performance in 1954 in Chicago, Illinois.

CHAPTER 1

EARLY ARTISTS

In the first half of the 1900s, US segregation made it illegal for Black people to perform in certain venues. Black musicians were often paid less than white musicians, and breaking through in music was more difficult for them. But many found a way.

OPERATIC LEGEND

Racism prevented opera singer Marian Anderson from performing in the US. She moved to Europe and wowed audiences with her voice to become an international star.

On April 9, 1939, Anderson made gains for civil rights when she performed at the Lincoln Memorial in Washington, DC. Although segregation made it illegal for Black and white people to use the same schools, restaurants, and more, both Black and white people went to the concert. More than seventy-five thousand people attended. Anderson continued singing during the civil rights movement and was a powerful voice for many years.

Anderson sings to a crowd at the Lincoln Memorial in Washington, DC, in 1939.

REFLECT

How do you think racism plays a role in shaping the music of Black artists?

SATCHMO BLOWS

Louis Armstrong was one of the most popular entertainers in the world in the 1940s and 1950s. An influential figure in jazz, his songs appeared on the radio and in movies. Born in New Orleans, Louisiana, the trumpeter and singer was nicknamed Satchmo.

In 1964 his song "Hello, Dolly!" reached the top of the charts. It made Armstrong the oldest artist, at sixty-two, to reach No. 1. "Hello, Dolly!" was added to the Grammy Hall of Fame in 2001.

> "If you have to ask what jazz is, you'll never know."
>
> —LOUIS ARMSTRONG,
> trumpeter and jazz legend

Armstrong playing his trumpet in 1951

ROCK'S GODMOTHER

Sister Rosetta Tharpe played a major role in the birth of rock and roll. Tharpe mixed jazz, gospel, and blues to create a unique sound. She also experimented on guitar during a time when female guitarists were rare.

Tharpe's songs "Rock Me" and "Strange Things Happening Every Day" are often considered some of the first rock songs.

Tharpe sings while playing the guitar in 1957.

DID YOU KNOW?

Jazz pianist and singer Nat King Cole won a Grammy many years after his death in 1965. In 1991 his daughter, Natalie Cole, used his recording of "Unforgettable" to create a duet. The song won four Grammy Awards.

In 1992 Natalie Cole holds the Grammy Award given for her and her father's duet of "Unforgettable."

Berry Gordy created Motown Records in 1959. Gordy is pictured here in 1970.

CHAPTER 2
OUTSIDE THE BOX

In 1959 small-time songwriter Berry Gordy took a chance when he created the record label Motown Records. Thanks to stars like Smokey Robinson and the Supremes, Motown was an instant success. Gordy thought outside of the box, like these artists, and created something unforgettable.

INNER VISIONS

Stevie Wonder is one of the most gifted artists in music history. The blind artist was a child prodigy. He signed a contract with Motown when he was only eleven.

Wonder created a series of groundbreaking records in the 1970s that showcased his talent. He explored new instruments and technologies and had hits like "Superstition" and "Sir Duke." He has won twenty-five Grammy Awards, including three Album of the Year honors.

Wonder performing in the 1970s

DID YOU KNOW?

Between 1961 and 1971, Motown produced 110 top 10 hits on the *Billboard* Top 100 list. The *Billboard* chart tracks the most popular songs each week.

THE HIGH PRIESTESS OF SOUL

Nina Simone's music told vivid stories and captured audiences. The pianist and singer didn't fit in one genre. Her music touched on jazz, folk, and soul. By the 1960s, her music connected with the civil rights movement.

   Some of Simone's songs, including "Strange Fruit," talked about issues in society, like racism and sexism. Simone never stopped putting this kind of material on her records. She never achieved mainstream pop success, but her legacy as a singer and storyteller is unmatched.

REFLECT

In what ways do you think a person's environment or experience impacts their music? How does where you live and your past experiences impact you?

Simone in 1977

SOUL BROTHER

James Brown's talent changed the way soul music was seen and heard back in the 1960s and 1970s. And his music continues to form the backbone of hip-hop. The Hardest Working Man in Show Business used his drive to create seventeen No. 1 R&B singles.

Brown and his band would perform for hours. Fans loved Brown's music. So do modern music producers. Brown and his band have been sampled in other songs more than seventy-four hundred times! The song "Funky Drummer" alone has been sampled more than fifteen hundred times.

James Brown at a concert in France in 1971

CHAPTER 3
SUPERSTAR ERA

B lack music exploded beginning in the 1970s. A new generation of superstars was born.

> "Music changes, and I'm going to change right along with it."
>
> —ARETHA FRANKLIN,
> in an interview in 1968

QUEEN OF SOUL

Aretha Franklin started her career as a gospel artist but became an R&B powerhouse in the 1960s thanks to songs like "Respect" and "Think." A radio DJ gave her the name the Queen of Soul. It stuck for the rest of Franklin's career.

Franklin was one of several R&B singers who crossed over and achieved mainstream success. She was able to sing pop, R&B, jazz, and even opera. Her songs have been in movies, and she performed at Barack Obama's presidential inauguration in 2009. Franklin continued singing and recording songs until her death in 2018.

Franklin sings during Obama's inauguration ceremony in 2009.

PURPLE REIGN

From writing hit songs for himself and other artists to playing the guitar unlike anyone else, Prince became a star on his own terms. Starting with hits like "Little Red Corvette," Prince conquered movies and TV for over thirty years as both an actor and musician. The Minneapolis, Minnesota, native (and lover of purple) was one of music's most recognizable stars. He was also one of the most talented, often playing every instrument on his tracks.

Prince sold more than 150 million records in his career. And many consider his Super Bowl performance in 2007 to be the greatest halftime show ever.

On April 26, 2008, Prince performs at the Coachella Valley Music and Arts Festival.

THE VOICE

Whitney Houston was born to sing. Her first two albums hit the top of the charts and are among the best-selling albums of all time. She is the only artist to have seven straight No. 1 singles (from 1985 to 1988).

In 1992 Houston moved into acting and her song "I Will Always Love You" became a major hit. More than twenty million copies have been sold. Many people consider Houston to be one of the greatest singers of all time.

Houston singing in 1988

QUEEN B

Beyoncé started her musical career as a child and became famous in the 1990s as the lead singer of Destiny's Child. The group was one of the most successful music groups of all time.

Beyoncé (*center*) performs with other Destiny's Child members Kelly Rowland (*left*) and Michelle Williams (*right*) in 2005.

After going solo in 2003, Beyoncé experienced even greater success. Songs like "Single Ladies (Put a Ring on It)" and "Crazy in Love" made her an international superstar. Her first five albums went to No. 1, and she starred in several movies. She continues to explore new musical sounds.

Beyoncé gives a performance at the Global Citizen Festival in 2018 in South Africa.

REFLECT

Music has changed over time. How does music from the past impact modern music? Do you notice similarities and differences?

DJ Kool Herc in 2009 at the event Bring Out the Sound System: The West Indian Roots of Hip Hop

CHAPTER 4

RAP AND BEYOND

In the 1970s, a new sound emerged from New York. The young Jamaican DJ Kool Herc experimented with records and discovered how to switch between the same record using two turntables. His breakbeats, a form of electronic music that uses drum breaks, were the start of hip-hop.

Hip-hop culture is found everywhere, and rap is a dominant musical genre. Black artists have found a creative outlet and broken boundaries within rap.

KINGS OF ROCK

The first major rap group was Run-DMC. The group featured two rappers—Joseph Simmons and Darryl McDaniels—and DJ Jason Mizell. The trio released their debut in 1983. Run-DMC achieved many firsts, including the first platinum rap record and the first rap Grammy nomination.

Run-DMC achieved a major milestone when it collaborated with the rock group Aerosmith. Their song "Walk This Way" was a major hit. In 2016 Run-DMC achieved another first when they became the first rap group to win the Grammy Lifetime Achievement Award.

Run-DMC giving a performance outside in the 1980s

DID YOU KNOW?

Three-time Grammy Award winner Lizzo is a talented rapper, singer, and songwriter. But she's also a classically trained flute player. Her instrument even has its own Instagram account.

Lizzo sings at the 2020 Brit Awards in London, England.

MR. PULITZER

Rap often explores a tough reality. Many rappers use harsh language to describe difficult situations. But it reflects their truth. Kendrick Lamar is one of today's most influential rappers. His music explores his life growing up in Compton, California. His clever use of wordplay has drawn raves from critics and fans.

Lamar performs during the Pepsi Super Bowl LVI Halftime Show.

Lamar won a 2017 Pulitzer Prize for one of his albums. The Pulitzer is an award for achievement in the arts. Lamar's win marked the first time a rap record won the honor. The Pulitzer committee cited Lamar for "capturing the complexity of modern African American life."

MIXING GENRES

Artists take different roads to find success. For Lil Nas X, it was a song that didn't fit neatly into a box. His "Old Town Road" mixed country and rap to create a catchy tune. It was the No. 1 song in the US for nineteen weeks.

The song propelled Lil Nas X to stardom. Along the way, he has defied stereotypes. He is a gay man, a rarity in rap. Lil Nas X tries to promote a positive message of acceptance. He is among the next generation of rap stars.

REFLECT

Many artists learn from previous artists and find inspiration from them.
Who inspires you and why?

FUTURE ARTISTS

The tradition of Black artists excelling in music, no matter the sound, continues proudly. Black musicians are making songs in all genres, from dance to country. Listen to the greatest Black musicians from the past and present, and learn about new artists to discover sounds you may like.

On December 10, 2021, Lil Nas X gives a concert in New York City.

GLOSSARY

debut: the first appearance of a musician

genre: a category of music characterized by a particular style

influential: having the power to affect another person or thing

platinum: a record that has sold more than one million copies

prodigy: a person with exceptional talent or ability

producer: a person who helps artists with their recording projects

sample: a portion of a song that is taken and reworked into another song

segregation: the separation of a race or class

single: a song that is released separately from an album but can also be a part of an album

turntable: the round plate that spins a record

SOURCE NOTES

8 "Quotes by Louis Armstrong," Louis Armstrong Society Jazz Band, accessed June 7, 2022, https://www.larmstrongsoc.org /quotes.

18 Norman Jopling, "Aretha Franklin Stops to Think—A Classic Interview from the Vaults," *Guardian* (US edition), March 20, 2012, https://www.theguardian.com/music/2012/mar/20 /aretha-franklin-classic-interview.

26 The 2018 Pulitzer Prize Winner in Music," Pulitzer Prizes, accessed June 7, 2022, https://www.pulitzer.org/winners /kendrick-lamar.

READ WOKE READING LIST

Britannica Kids: Soul Music
https://kids.britannica.com/students/article/soul-music
/606788

Celebrating Black Music Month
https://nmaahc.si.edu/explore/stories/celebrating-black
-music-month

Rolling Stone: The 200 Greatest Hip-Hop Albums of All Time
https://www.rollingstone.com/music/music-lists/best-hip
-hop-albums-1323916/

Shea, Therese. *Kendrick Lamar: Becoming the Voice of Compton.*
New York: Enslow, 2020.

Smith, Elliott. *Black Achievements in Arts and Literature:
Celebrating Gordon Parks, Amanda Gorman, and More.*
Minneapolis: Lerner Publications, 2024.

Todd, Traci N. *Nina: A Story of Nina Simone.* New York: G. P.
Putnam's Sons, 2021.

Wilkins, Ebony. *Beyoncé: Queen of the Spotlight.* New York:
Random House Children's Books, 2020.

INDEX

PHOTO ACKNOWLEDGMENTS

Image credits: Daniel Leal-Olivas/Alamy Stock Photo, p. 4; Doug Peters/Alamy Stock Photo, p. 5; Phillip Harrington/Alamy Stock Photo, p. 6; World History Archive/Alamy Stock Photo, p. 7; Pictorial Press/Alamy Stock Photo, pp. 9, 12; Mirrorpix/Alamy Stock Photo, p. 10; AP Photo/Gershoff/MediaPunch, p. 11; Media Punch/Alamy Stock Photo, pp. 13, 19; marka/eps/Alamy Stock Photo, p. 15; Philippe Gras/Alamy Stock Photo, p. 16; Michael Ochs Archives/Stringer/Getty Images, p. 17; Jason Reed/Alamy Stock Photo, p. 18; Dave Hogan/Hulton Archive/Getty Images, p. 20; Fabio Diena/Alamy Stock Photo, p. 21; Kevin Mazur/Getty Images Entertainment/Getty Images, p. 22; Michael Ochs Archives/Stringer/Getty Images, p. 24; AP Photo/Joel C Ryan, p. 25; AP Photo/Todd Rosenberg, p. 26; Kevin Kane/WireImage/Getty Images, p. 27. Design elements: Anastasiia Gevko/Shutterstock. Cicely Lewis portrait photos by Fernando Decillis.

Cover: AP Photo/Werner Kreusch (Louis Armstrong); AP Photo/Matt Sayles (Beyoncé).

Lerner Publications Company
An imprint of Lerner Publishing Group, Inc.
241 First Avenue North
Minneapolis, MN 55401 USA

For reading levels and more information, look up this title at www.lernerbooks.com.

Main body text set in Aptifer Sans LT Pro.
Typeface provided by Linotype AG.

Editor: Brianna Kaiser **Designer:** Kimberly Morales **Photo Editor:** Annie Zheng
Lerner team: Martha Kranes

Library of Congress Cataloging-in-Publication Data

Names: Smith, Elliott, 1976– author.
Title: Black achievements in music : celebrating Louis Armstrong, Beyoncé, and more / Elliott Smith.
Description: Minneapolis : Lerner Publications, 2023. | Series: Black excellence project (read woke books) | Includes bibliographical references and index. | Audience: Ages 9–14 | Audience: Grades 4–6 | Summary: "Black musicians have been innovative and created new sounds in many genres. Learn about Black people who have had tremendous impact on the music industry, including Nina Simone, Whitney Houston, and Kendrick Lamar"— Provided by publisher.
Identifiers: LCCN 2022033366 (print) | LCCN 2022033367 (ebook) | ISBN 9781728486581 (library binding) | ISBN 9781728496269 (ebook)
Subjects: LCSH: African American musicians—Biography—Juvenile literature. | LCGFT: Biographies.
Classification: LCC ML3929 .S65 2023 (print) | LCC ML3929 (ebook) | DDC 780.89/96073 [B]—dc23/eng/20220805

LC record available at https://lccn.loc.gov/2022033366
LC ebook record available at https://lccn.loc.gov/2022033367

Manufactured in the United States of America
1-52588-50762-10/31/2022